The Healthy Cat Food Cookbook

Delectable Homemade Meals & Treats for Your Feline Friend

By: Cynthia Cherry

Copyrights and Trademarks

Disclaimer and Legal Notice

Foreword

Every year there seems to be a new trend in the pet food industry. In recent years, countless pet parents have been making the switch to homemade cat food diets. Unfortunately, many of those who make the switch do not fully understand their pet's nutritional needs and they do not realize the importance of using a healthy and balanced pet food recipe. In many cases, this leads to malnutrition and other health problems for the pet which could have easily been avoided with a little research.

If you are thinking about switching your cat to a homemade cat food diet, do yourself and your cat a favor by learning as much as you can about the subject before you decide. Within the pages of this book you will receive an overview of your cat's nutritional needs as well as an introduction to the world of raw cat food and other homemade cat food diets. You will also receive detailed information about the pros and cons of homemade cat food as well as tips for creating a balanced cat food diet at home. Finally, you will receive a collection of recipes for homemade cat food and treats that you can make yourself if you decide that it is the best option.

If you are ready to learn more about homemade cat food, turn the page and keep reading!

Table of Contents

Introduction..1

Chapter One: Understanding Your Cat's Nutritional Needs3

    1. Macronutrients for Cats...4

        a.) Recommended Macronutrient Ratios 8

    2. Essential Vitamins and Minerals..............................9

    3. How Many Calories Does Your Cat Need?...............13

Chapter Two: Are All Commercial Cat Foods Bad? 17

    1.) How is Commercial Cat Food Made? 18

    2.) Different Types of Commercial Cat Food...................20

    3.) How to Read a Cat Food Label 26

        a.) AAFCO Statement of Nutritional Adequacy..........26

        b.) Guaranteed Analysis.....................................27

        c.) List of Ingredients 28

    4.) What are the Best Commercial Cat Foods? 31

Chapter Three: Different Types of Homemade Cat Food ...33

    1. Raw Meat and Bones..34

        a.) Sample Frankenprey Meal Plan 37

    2. Cooked Homemade Cat Food 38

Chapter Four: Risks and Rewards of Homemade Cat Food41

    1. Pros and Cons of Homemade Cat Food....................42

    2. Potential Risks and Safety Precautions 44

Chapter Five: A Raw Diet for Your Cat 47

1. The Components of Raw Cat Food Diets.....................48

2. Supplements for Raw Food Diets 50

3. Transitioning Your Cat Onto a Raw Food Diet............54

Chapter Six: Homemade Cat Food Recipes........................57

1. Tips for Portioning Homemade Cat Food 58

2. Raw Homemade Cat Food Recipes 60

Simple Raw Chicken Recipe 61

Ground Chicken and Eggs Dinner.................................61

Chopped Chicken and Veggies Recipe 62

Easy Ground Duck Dinner...63

Chopped Turkey and Pumpkin Recipe 65

Ground Beef and Bone Dinner 65

Turkey and Rabbit Recipe with Raw Bone...................66

Ground Rabbit Dinner with Bones 67

Reduced-Protein Turkey Dinner....................................68

Raw Chicken Recipe without Bone................................69

3. Cooked Homemade Cat Food Recipes........................70

High-Protein Chicken and Spinach Recipe 71

Sautéed Rabbit Stew..72

Reduced Protein Duck and Egg Recipe 73

Chicken and Broccoli Stew..73

Cornish Hen and Oat Dinner..74

Beefy Potato Cat Casserole..75

Creamy Salmon Pasta 76

Chicken, Lentils and Rice Recipe 77

Sardine and Chicken Liver Dinner 78

Turkey and Pasta Recipe 79

Chapter Seven: Homemade Treat Recipes 81

Tuna Cat Crackers..83

Catnip Kitty Cookies..83

Chicken Jerky Bites..84

Sunflower Oat Treats 85

Beefy Bites..86

Chicken Biscuits..87

Tasty Tuna Tidbits..87

Cheesy Cat Treats..88

Baked Liver Bites..89

Canned Food Cookies..90

Chapter Eight: Frequently Asked Questions......................91

Index..99

References..107

Introduction

If you are concerned about your cat's health and wellbeing, you may be considering making the switch to a homemade cat food diet. Homemade cat food is becoming increasingly more popular with each passing year, but many cat owners still do not have a thorough understanding of what it is and how it can benefit their cat. Before you make any significant changes to your cat's diet, it is very important that you understand the options as well as the pros and cons of the switch.

Homemade cat food can be very nutritious and it can provide a wide variety of benefits for your cat, but only if you use it right. Unfortunately, many cat owners do not realize that homemade cat food is not just something you can whip up on a whim – it needs to be complete and properly balanced in order to meet your cat's nutritional requirements. This isn't to say that you cannot make healthy cat food at home, but you need to understand the basics of cat nutrition and you need to start with a healthy and balanced recipe.

If you are considering switching your cat to a homemade cat food diet, this book is the perfect place for you to start. Within the pages of this book you will receive an overview of your cat's nutritional needs as well as an introduction to the world of raw cat food and other homemade cat food diets. You will also receive detailed information about the pros and cons of homemade cat food as well as tips for creating a balanced cat food diet at home. Finally, you will receive a collection of recipes for homemade cat food and treats that you can make yourself if you are willing.

If you are ready to learn more about homemade cat food and to determine whether it might be a good choice for your cat, turn the page and keep reading!

Chapter One: Understanding Your Cat's Nutritional Needs

In order to decide whether or not a homemade cat food diet will meet your cat's nutritional needs, you first need to cultivate an understanding of what those needs are. Cats need many of the same essential nutrients as humans but in very different ratios. If you do not choose a diet that is properly formulated for cats, your cat could end up suffering from nutritional deficiencies or other health problems. In this chapter you will receive an overview of cat nutrition to help you decide whether switching to homemade cat food might benefit your cat.

1. Macronutrients for Cats

The first thing you need to understand about cat nutrition is that cats are obligate carnivores – this means that their bodies are designed to derive nutrition primarily from animal products, not plant products. Meat plays a key role in your cat's nutrition, though it is not the only source of nutrition you should be thinking about. Like all living things, cats require a balance of the three main nutrients (called macronutrients) as well as certain levels of lesser nutrients like vitamins and minerals (called micronutrients). The three macronutrients that all living things need are protein, fat, and carbohydrate. You will find an overview of each of these macronutrients in the following pages.

Protein

This macronutrient is made up of amino acids which form the building blocks of healthy muscle and tissue. Protein is the most important nutritional consideration for cats because it plays a key role in maintaining essential biological functions. Protein also provides your cat's body with the carbon chains needed to produce glucose to be used for energy. For cats, protein should come from meat, fish, and eggs.

There are twenty-two different amino acids that cats need to maintain healthy bodily function. Your cat's body is capable of synthesizing (producing) eleven of those amino acids – the other eleven must come from dietary sources. The amino acids your cat's body cannot produce on his own are called "essential amino acids". <u>For cats, the eleven essential amino acids are</u>:

- Argentine
- Histidine
- Isoleucine
- Leucine
- Lysine
- Methionine
- Phenylalanine
- Taurine
- Threonine
- Tryptophan
- Valine

Not only is protein very important for cats because it is what their bodies are designed to digest, but certain amino acids can ONLY come from animal sources – this includes arginine and taurine. It is also important to note that most animal proteins are also complete proteins. A complete protein is one which contains all of the eleven essential amino acids. Most animal products like meat, poultry, fish, and eggs are complete proteins.

Fat

After protein, dietary fat is the second most important nutritional consideration for cats. Fat is a highly concentrated source of energy and it contains essential fatty acids that your cat's body needs to help transport and utilize key nutrients. Fats can be derived from both plant and animal sources but, as is the case with protein, animal-based fats are more biologically valuable to your cat than plant-based sources. This simply means that they are easier for your cat's body to digest, absorb, and utilize.

Fatty acids help to maintain healthy cell structure and function in your cat's body – they also help to transport fat-soluble vitamins throughout the body. Fats also play an important role in keeping your cat's skin and coat healthy – you can tell that a cat doesn't have enough fat in its diet if its coat is dull and rough. Cats need both omega-3 and omega-6 fatty acids in their diet. Some omega-3 fatty acids include alpha-linolenic acid (ALA), eicosapentaenoic acid (EPA), and docosahexaenoic acid (DHA). The four omega-6 fatty acids include linoleic acid (LA), gamma linolenic acid (GLA), dihomo-gamma-linolenic acid (DGLA) and arachidonic acid (AA).

Like amino acids, essential fatty acids are those that your cat cannot synthesize on his own so they must come from his diet. In terms of how much your cat needs of these essential fatty acids, research is still being conducted but current recommendations for the ratio of omega-6 to omega-3 fatty acids for cats are between 10:1 and 5:1. Many commercial cat foods have high levels of omega-6 fatty acids and they actually add omega-3 supplements to help lower the ratio. If you choose to make your own homemade cat food, you will need to make sure that these fatty acids are properly balanced.

Carbohydrate

For humans, the typical American diet is very carbohydrate-centered. For many people, the typical meal consists largely of grains or starchy foods (like rice, pasta, or bread) with some kind of meat and perhaps a side dish of vegetables. The human body is designed to effectively process carbohydrates and to break them down into glucose molecules which can be used immediately for energy. Your cat's body is not designed this way – in fact, cats have no biological requirement for carbohydrates in their diet. The only carbohydrates that wild cats eat come from the stomach contents of their prey.

Given this information, it should be easy to see the problem with many commercial cat foods that are largely made up of grains and other carbohydrates with meat playing a secondary role. Although cats do not have any specific requirements for carbohydrate in their diet, carbs do offer some nutritional benefit. Cats can derive a limited amount of energy from carbs and they also provide dietary fiber which helps to support a healthy digestive system. It is important to ensure, however, that any carbohydrate your cat does get from his diet is easily digestible.

a.) Recommended Macronutrient Ratios

Now that you have a better understanding of the three key macronutrients your cat needs, you may be wondering exactly how much of each he should get in his diet. Different pet experts and animal nutritionists will give you different values but The Waltham Centre for Pet Nutrition suggests a macronutrient ratio for cats of 50% protein, 40% fat, and 10% carbohydrate. Remember, both protein and fats should come from animal-based sources like meat, fish, poultry, and eggs.

Plant-based sources of protein or fat are not necessarily bad for your cat but they should only be included on a supplemental basis. For carbohydrates, remember that less is more – 10% is a maximum for how much carbohydrate should be in your cat's diet. The best carbohydrates for cats are complex carbs like oats, barley, sweet potatoes, and chickpeas. Cooking these foods makes them more digestible for cats as well. Be sure to avoid low-quality carbs like grain by-products, gluten, middlings, and mill run products.

2. Essential Vitamins and Minerals

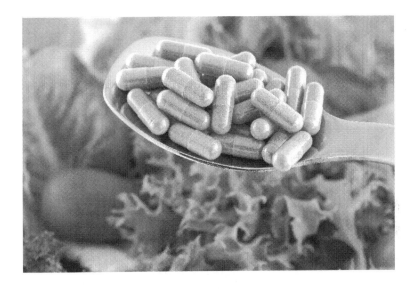

The three key nutrients (protein, fat, and carbohydrate) are known as macronutrients and the remaining nutrients (vitamins and minerals) are called micronutrients. These nutrients are just as important in your cat's diet, but the amount he needs for these nutrients is much smaller. A vitamin is an inorganic compound that helps with your cat's metabolic activities. Similar to proteins and fatty acids, there are certain vitamins that your cat's body cannot synthesize so they must come from his diet – vitamin deficiencies can cause serious health problems for your cat.

Below you will find a chart outlining the essential vitamins your cat needs, their function, and how much he should be getting on a daily basis:

Vitamin	Function	Daily Allowance
Vitamin A	Immunity, vision, growth, fetal development	63 µg
Vitamin D	Skeletal structure, phosphorus balance	0.4 µg
Vitamin E	Defense against oxidative damage	2.5 mg
Vitamin K	Activation of clotting factors and bone proteins	82 µg
Vitamin B$_1$ (thiamin)	Metabolism of energy and carbohydrate	
Riboflavin	Enzyme function	0.27 mg
Vitamin B$_6$	Generation of glucose, red blood cell function, immune response, hormone regulation	0.16 mg
Niacin	Enzyme function	2.5 mg
Pantothenic Acid	Energy metabolism	0.4 mg

Vitamin B$_{12}$	Enzyme function	1.4 µg
Folic Acid	Amino acid metabolism, protein synthesis	47 µg

Minerals are another type of micronutrient and there are twelve of them that are considered essential for cats. Phosphorus and calcium are necessary for strong bones and teeth while other minerals help to facilitate nerve impulse transmission, muscle contractions, and cell signaling. Your cat's need for certain minerals may change as he grows and matures but the basics of essential minerals for cats are described in the chart below:

Mineral	**Function**	**Daily Allowance**
Calcium	Forming bones and teeth, nerve impulse transmission, muscle contraction, cell signaling	0.18 g
Phosphorus	Skeletal structure, energy metabolism, DNA/RNA structure	0.16 g
Magnesium	Enzyme function, hormone secretion, structure of bones and teeth	25 mg

Sodium	Acid-base balance, regulating osmotic pressure, nerve impulse generation and transmission	42 mg
Potassium	Nerve impulse transmission, enzyme reactions, transport functions, acid-base balance	0.33 g
Chlorine	Fluid osmolarity, acid-base balance	60 mg
Iron	Energy metabolism, synthesis of hemoglobin and myoglobin	5 mg
Copper	Iron metabolism, connective tissue formation, blood cell formation, defense against oxidative damage	0.3 mg
Zinc	Enzyme reactions, protein and carb metabolism, skin function, healing	4.6 mg
Manganese	Bone development, enzyme reaction, neurological function	0.3 mg

Selenium	Defense against oxidative damage, immune response	19 µg
Iodine	Cell differentiation, growth and development regulation of metabolic rate	88 µg

3. How Many Calories Does Your Cat Need?

In addition to understanding the nutrients your cat needs, you also need to be aware of his calorie needs. A calorie is simply a unit of energy derived from food. Your cat's daily calorie needs will change over the course of his life and it will be impacted by several factors such as:

- Age and Sex
- Weight
- Activity Level
- Intact/Altered
- Pregnant/Lactating

When they are very young, kittens have very high needs for energy. During the first few weeks of life, a kitten needs about 20 to 25 calories per 100 grams of bodyweight. After a few weeks the kittens will start to wean themselves off their mother's milk at which point you need to start feeding them kitten food. The daily calorie needs for a 5-pound kitten is about 200 calories.

It is also important to note that pregnant/lactating female cats also have high needs for energy – about 600 calories per day for a 10-pound cat, 850 for a 15-pound cat, and upwards of 1,000 calories a day for a 20-pound cat. Keep in mind that most female cats lose weight during nursing no matter how much you feed them. Just do your best to ensure that she gains enough weight during the pregnancy (an increase of 40% to 50%) so she has enough stored energy to sustain herself.

For the average housecat, 170 calories a day is adequate for a 5-pound cat and a 10-pound cat needs about 280 calories. For a 15-pound cat, 360 is the magic number and a 20-pound cat needs about 440 calories. If your cat is very overweight you need to be intentional about how much you are feeding him. You need to make sure that his basic needs for nutrition and energy are met without giving him too many extra calories. If your cat is overweight at 10 pounds, feed him 240 calories. If he is overweight at 15-pound, feed him 280 calories a day – for 20-pound overweight cats, feed 440 calories.

Just because your cat weighs 20 pounds doesn't mean that he is overweight or obese. In order to determine whether your cat's weight is healthy or unhealthy you need to take a look at his condition. If your cat feels bony with little to no fat covering the ribs he could be underweight. Over your cat has obvious fat deposits along the back, in the fact, and on the legs, he could be overweight. An obvious rounding of the belly or distension of the abdomen are also signs of overweight in cats. The ideal weight for cats will appear in the form of a moderate waistline behind the ribs and a thin layer of fat over the ribs.

Chapter Two: Are All Commercial Cat Foods Bad?

Now that you have a deeper understanding of your cat's nutritional needs, you may be wondering whether his current food meets those needs. Pet owners often do not realize it, but many of the pet foods they see on pet store shelves are made with low-quality ingredients that do not provide pets with the complete nutrition they need to be healthy. But are all commercial pet foods bad? In this chapter you will learn about how commercial pet foods are made and you will receive an overview of the different types of food and how to tell good from bad.

1.) How is Commercial Cat Food Made?

When you open up a bag of commercial dry cat food all you see is kibbles – you probably won't see anything that looks even remotely like the fresh ingredients listed on the label. The reason for this is that dry commercial pet foods are processed and cooked in a way that the final result is a cohesive product that is cut into bite-sized pieces. <u>The process through which dry cat food is made is called extrusion and it involves several key steps – you will find an overview of these steps below</u>:

Step 1: Assemble the Ingredients

The first stage in the process is to gather and store the individual raw ingredients to be used in the pet food. For commercial cat foods, these raw ingredients usually consist of fresh meats, meat meals, fats, grains, other carbohydrates and nutritional supplements.

Step 2: Grind the Materials

After the ingredients have all been assembled they must be ground into smaller pieces to prepare them for cooking. For some ingredients (like grains), grinding them up actually makes the nutrients easier for your cat's body to digest and to absorb.

Step 3: Mix the Ingredients

Once the ingredients have been gathered and ground, they are blended in specific proportions according to the cat food recipe. Many cat food manufacturers produce batches of 2,000 pounds of cat food at a time, though there are some high-quality brands that cook their foods in small batches in order to ensure quality.

Step 4: Knead the Dough

When the ingredients are mixed together they form a sort of dough that is then kneaded by forcing it through a machine called an extruder. This machine combines the dough with the right amount of moisture while cooking, shaping, and cutting it concurrently with the cooking process.

Step 5: Cool and Dry

Once the food has been cooked and cut, it must be cooled and dried at just the right rate to prevent mold growth and to prevent the product from becoming crumbly.

Step 6: Coating with Flavor

Many commercial pet food manufactures do something called "enrobing" to their final product – this involves spraying or coating the kibbles in powder to enhance the flavor and to boost the shelf-life of the product.

This is the basic formula for the production of commercial dry cat food. Different companies may follow a slightly difference process or they may skip some steps entirely. In the next section you will learn the basics about different types of commercial cat food.

2.) *Different Types of Commercial Cat Food*

When you walk into your local pet store you are probably greeted by a seemingly endless assortment of pet food products. Not only do most pet stores carry many different brands, but most brands offer multiple formulas. With so many options to select from, how do you make a good choice? The first stage in the process for choosing a quality cat food is to learn the difference between the main types of cat food. Here are some of the most popular types of commercial cat food:

- Traditional Dry Kibble
- Canned and Wet Food
- Grain-Free Food
- Holistic Cat Food
- Raw/Fresh Cat Food
- Dehydrated Food
- Freeze-Dried Cat Food

To help you understand the differences between these types of cat food you will find an overview of each type below:

Traditional Dry Kibble

This is the most popular and also the most affordable type of commercial cat food. Most kibbles are made using the extrusion process described in the last section, though there are other production methods out there such as air-drying, dehydrating, and freeze-drying. Kibble generally has the longest shelf-life of any commercial cat food product and the hard pieces can help to scrape plaque and tartar off your cat's teeth as he chews.

One thing to be aware of with traditional kibble is that cooking the raw ingredients at high temperatures (often as high as 400°F) can destroy the active enzymes as well as a significant portion of the nutritional content of the raw ingredients. This is why many kibbles are fortified with nutritional supplements – they are included to replace the natural nutrients that were lost during cooking.

Canned and Wet Food

Commercial canned cat foods are made in a slightly different way than traditional kibbles. The raw ingredients are still assembled and then cut into smaller pieces then they are cooked in the broth or gravy that will keep the product moist. After cooking, the product is packed into cans or pouches and then the containers are sealed and sterilized using heat. The sterilization process for wet cat food negates the need for as many food preservatives that are often found in dry foods.

Wet and canned food for cats comes in a variety of different forms including paté, shredded pieces, stew-like mixtures, chunks of meat in gravy, and more. This type of food has a much higher moisture content than dry cat food. In order to compare the nutritional content of wet foods to dry foods, you must first convert the guaranteed analysis to a dry matter basis. Simply subtract the moisture content as a percentage from 100 then divide that number by the percentage of the value you want to find.

For example, for a wet food with 82% moisture and 9.5% protein you would subtract 82 from 100 to get a dry matter percentage of 18%. Then, divide the 9.5% by the 18% and you are left with 52.8% dry matter protein. You can take this number and compare it directly to the percentage of crude protein on a dry cat food label.

Grain-Free Food

This type of cat food is available in both dry and wet form – it just uses different ingredients than traditional canned food and kibble. Many low-quality pet food manufacturers use corn, wheat, and soy ingredients to bulk up their products without increasing their costs. Unfortunately, many grains and other carbohydrates offer limited nutritional value for cats so the food as a whole loses a great deal of its nutritional integrity. Grain-free cat food uses grain-free carbohydrates like tapioca starch, chickpeas, green peas, and sweet potatoes to provide dietary fiber and other healthy nutrients without using any grains.

Holistic Cat Food

The term "holistic" is not regulated by the FDA or by the American Association of Feed Control Officials (AAFCO) so pet food manufacturers are free to use this term as they like. The conventional definition of the term according to Merriam-Webster, however, is "relating to or concerned with wholes or with complete systems rather than the analysis of, treatment of, or dissection into parts".

Essentially, holistic cat food is designed to nourish the cat's whole body, not just to fill his stomach. Holistic cat foods use high-quality, all-natural ingredients that not only meet your cat's nutritional needs but they also help to support his whole body health by boosting his immune system, supporting healthy digestion, protecting his bones and joints, and improving his skin and coat condition. Though there are exceptions to every rule, holistic cat foods are, for the most part, high-quality cat foods.

Raw/Fresh Cat Food

Within the last decade or so, several pet food manufacturers have started to offer raw or fresh cat food products. These products are made with fresh ingredients and they are either completely raw or just lightly cooked. Raw and fresh cat foods come in several different forms including rolls that can be sliced for serving, chunks, or pre-shaped patties. This type of cat food tends to be fairly expensive and it needs to be kept refrigerated or frozen.

Dehydrated Food

This type of cat food is not cooked in the same way as traditional kibbles – it is cooked, but not to extremely high temperatures. After the ingredients are assembled they are exposed to a consistent level of heat which removes the moisture from the ingredients. In some cases this heating process might change the shape or texture of the ingredients and it can change the nutritional content as well, but not to the same degree as traditional kibble. Dehydrated food is also fairly expensive but it is also very good for your cat.

Freeze-Dried Cat Food

Similar to dehydrated cat food, freeze-dried cat food has had all of the moisture removed but the process to accomplish this is different. First the food is flash-frozen and then the food is exposed to a strong vacuum to remove the moisture content while the ingredients are still frozen. This method preserves almost all of the nutritional content of the raw ingredients and the enzymes in the food are suspended until the product is rehydrated for feeding.

3.) How to Read a Cat Food Label

When you look at a bag of cat food you will probably see some pretty pictures of fresh ingredients, maybe a happy cat. You might also see some words like "delicious" or "natural flavor". It is marketing gimmicks like this that confuse and mislead pet parents – it is things like this that make the process of picking a high-quality cat food so difficult. But if you can learn to sift through the smoke and mirrors, cutting down to the basics and the raw facts you can learn how to tell a good cat food from a bad one in just a few minutes.

a.) AAFCO Statement of Nutritional Adequacy

Though pet food is not as closely regulated as human food by the FDA, there are still some rules in place. The American Association of Feed Control Officials (AAFCO) is responsible for regulating the manufacture and production of pet foods and animal feed. Through research and feeding trials, AAFCO has come up with a nutrient profile for dogs and cats in various life stages – growth and development (puppies and kittens) and maintenance (adult). These nutrient profiles provide minimum requirements for key nutrients such as protein, fat, vitamins and minerals that cat food needs to meet in order to be considered "complete and balanced".

When reading a cat food label, the first thing you want to look for is an AAFCO statement of nutritional adequacy. If the product meets the minimum nutritional requirements for cats in the designated life stage as determined by AAFCO's nutrient profiles, the package will bear a statement that looks something like this:

"[Product Name] is formulated to meet the nutritional levels established by the AAFCO Cat Food Nutrient Profiles"

If the pet food product you are looking at carries this statement you can rest assured that it will meet your cat's basic nutritional needs. If it doesn't have this statement, you should move on to another product. Keep in mind, however, that just because a product meets the minimum nutritional requirements for cats doesn't mean that it is a high-quality product, you still have to look at the guaranteed analysis and the ingredients list.

b.) Guaranteed Analysis

The guaranteed analysis for a pet food product shows the percentage of key nutrients on a dry matter basis – this includes crude protein, crude fat, crude fiber and moisture.

This portion of the pet food label is a good part to use when making a direct comparison between two dry cat foods. Remember, the recommended macronutrient ratios for cats is 50% protein, 40% fat, and 10% carbohydrate. So, when looking at the guaranteed analysis for two products you want to choose the one with the higher protein and fat percentages and the lowest crude fiber percentage. To determine the dry matter value for these percentages, use the same formula that was described for wet cat food. You can also find a dry matter basis calculator online that will allow you to just plug in your numbers.

c.) List of Ingredients

After taking a look at the guaranteed analysis for the product your final step is to review the list of ingredients. The ingredients lists for pet food products are organized in descending order by volume. This means that the ingredients at the top of the list are present in the highest volume. Keep in mind, however, that the weight of ingredients is generally calculated before cooking – items that have a high moisture content (like fresh meat or fish) will be much lower in volume after the moisture has been cooked out of them. The exception to this rule is meat meals (like chicken meal).

Meat meals have already been cooked down to a moisture content around 10% so their volume will not change significantly during cooking. This means that meat meals are actually a much more highly concentrated source of protein than fresh meat. You want to be careful, however, about what kind of meat meal is in the product. Named sources like chicken meal or turkey meal are considered high-quality additions but unnamed meat meal (like poultry meal) or by-product meals are not. As a general rule, you should avoid pet food products that are made with by-products because you don't know where they came from and you can't judge their quality.

When reading the ingredients list for pet foods you want to see at least one high-quality source of animal protein listed at the top. Again, fresh meats are a good option but meat meals are more concentrated in terms of protein content by volume. Avoid any products that list a carbohydrate first, especially if it is made with corn, wheat, or soy. As a general rule you want to avoid ingredients that offer little to no nutritional value – this is true for most corn, wheat, and soy ingredients as well as other low-quality fillers like gluten, middlings, and grain by-products.

In addition to checking for high-quality proteins, you should also look for animal fats like salmon oil or chicken fat. Remember, fat is a highly concentrated source of energy for cats and it provides essential fatty acids. An ingredient like chicken fat may not sound appetizing for you, but it is a valuable addition to commercial cat food. Plant-based fats like flaxseed or canola oil are not necessarily bad for your cat but they are less biologically valuable than animal-based fats. If the product has at least one animal fat it is perfectly fine for it to include some plant-based fats as well.

In terms of carbohydrates in commercial cat foods, you want to make sure that they are high-quality and digestible sources. Complex carbs like whole-grain brown rice, oatmeal, and barley are good options, as are gluten-free and grain-free options like sweet potatoes, tapioca starch, green peas, and chickpeas. Avoid any product that seems to include a large number of carbohydrate sources, even if they are of high quality because cats can only digest so much carbohydrate. Too much carbohydrate in a cat's diet can lead to bloating, gas, diarrhea, and other potential digestive issues.

4.) What are the Best Commercial Cat Foods?

When it comes to commercial cat foods there are dozens, perhaps even hundreds of different brands to choose from and many pet food brands offer a wide variety of different recipes. By using the information in the last chapter you can make a comparison between two pet food products to determine which one is the better buy. If you just want to know which cat food brands are the best, however, here is a list of commercial cat food manufacturers that generally product high-quality food products for cats:

- Acana
- Addiction
- Blue Buffalo

- Canidae
- Castor & Pollux
- Earthborn Holistic

- Fromm
- Holistic Select
- Honest Kitchen
- I and Love and You
- Merrick
- Natural Balance
- Nature's Variety
- Nutro

- Orijen
- Organix
- Primal Pet Foods
- Stella & Chewy's
- Taste of the Wild
- Wellness
- Wysong
- Ziwipeak

**This list is by no means complete but it will give you a good idea where to start if you want to find a high-quality commercial pet food for your cat.

Chapter Three: Different Types of Homemade Cat Food

Now that you know a little bit more about the different kinds of commercial cat food you are ready to learn about homemade cat food diets. What makes homemade cat food better than commercial cat food and what kind of ingredients go into a homemade diet? You will learn the answers to these questions and more in this chapter. By learning this information you will be able to make a more informed decision regarding whether a homemade diet is the right choice for your cat.

1. Raw Meat and Bones

When it comes to homemade cat food there are many proponents for a completely raw diet. Do not misunderstand this type of diet – a raw diet for cats consists of more than just raw meat and it may include some partially cooked ingredients. The ideal raw diet for cats is made up of 80% to 85% raw meat, 5% to 10% raw organ meats (half of which is liver), and the remaining 10% is made up of raw edible bones.

If you really want to get into the details of raw diets for cats, there are three primary methodologies that are used to prepare homemade diets: whole prey, grinding, and frankenprey. The latter two follow the rules mentioned earlier – they follow an 80/10/5/5 rule which goes into a little more detail than the rule stated above. Both the grinding and frankenprey methodologies advocate for 80% to 87% fresh meat, skin, fat, sinew, and connective tissues with 5% to 10% edible bone, 3% to 5% liver, and 5% from other organ meats.

The whole prey methodology is as close to the natural diet of wild cats as you can get without making your cat catch his own dinner. The exact origins of this methodology are unknown but it is known that rodents consist of roughly 4% liver and 5% bone. Rabbits contain less than 4% liver and a little less than 10% bone and wild birds have even lower percentages. It would seem that the whole prey methodology is a combination of the values for the typical wild feline diet.

The grinding methodology is one of the most popular methods. It follows the 80/10/5/5 rule but the ingredients are all ground together using a meat grinder – this makes the food very easy for the cat to chew and to digest. It is also worth noting that grinding the raw food makes the texture and consistency very similar to canned cat foods which can help picky eaters transition onto a raw food diet. The frankenprey method also followed the 80/10/5/5 rule but the cat is fed measured amount of different animal parts over the course of a week instead of feeding a cohesive product every day.

The frankenprey methodology is gaining in popularity, though it is still not as well-known as the grinding method. The benefit of the frankenprey methodology is that it approximates the way cats eat in the wild – they eat different animals as they catch them so their diet is balanced as a whole, even if each individual meal is not complete in terms of nutrition. The meals for the frankenprey methodology are usually a mix of meat, bones, and organs (some can be all meat) and they are fed in larger chunks that the cat has to chew up to eat.

There are many benefits associated with the frankenprey methodology, most of them due to how closely it approximates the natural diet of wild cats. By feeding the diet in large chunks the cat has to actively engage with the meal and the process of chewing provides mental as well as physical challenges for the cat. The main benefit, however, is that the process of gnawing raw meat and bones helps to keep the cat's teeth clean and free from plaque and tartar. This type of diet will not repair prior dental damage or remove accumulated tartar but it will prevent the condition from progressing.

The whole prey method of feeding raw food to cats is the closest to their natural diet but it is the least known of the three main methodologies. To use this methodology you literally feed your cat whole animals like rats, mice, and young chicks. This diet offers great nutritional advantages but there are many challenges involved. Some cat owners have trouble handling dead animals and many cats that are used to a commercial diet fail to recognize the animals as food. It may take time to transition onto this type of diet but it can be very beneficial for cats.

a.) Sample Frankenprey Meal Plan

If you choose to follow the frankenprey methodology for raw cat food you will need to follow a specific feeding schedule to ensure that your cat gets a balanced diet. You can feel free to change the order of the meals listed in this sample meal plan but try not to make too many changes as it is already properly balanced.

Day	Breakfast	Lunch	Dinner
Monday	5 oz. each chicken, duck, turkey heart	3 bone-in chicken wings, 7 oz. chicken ribs w/ meat, 7 oz. small rabbit bones w/ meat	5 oz. rabbit meat
Tuesday	5 oz. chopped beef round	3 oz. liver, 3 oz. gizzards	½ turkey drumstick
Wednesday	5 oz. each chicken, duck, turkey heart	3 bone-in chicken wings, 7 oz. chicken ribs w/ meat, 7 oz. small rabbit bones w/ meat	½ chicken leg quarter
Thursday	5 oz. chopped pork loin	3 oz. kidney, 3 oz. chicken breast meat	5 oz. rabbit meat
Friday	5 oz. each	3 oz. liver, 3 oz.	4 chicken wing

	chicken, duck, turkey heart	gizzards ½ can sardines	drummettes (bone and skin)
Saturday	5 oz. chopped beef round	3 bone-in chicken wings, 7 oz. chicken ribs w/ meat, 7 oz. small rabbit bones w/ meat	½ turkey drumstick Egg whites
Sunday	5 oz. chopped pork loin	3 oz. kidney, 3 oz. chicken breast meat	½ chicken leg quarter

**The portions listed in this meal plan are enough to feed three adult cats on a daily basis. If you have one or two cats you will need to scale the portions.

2. Cooked Homemade Cat Food

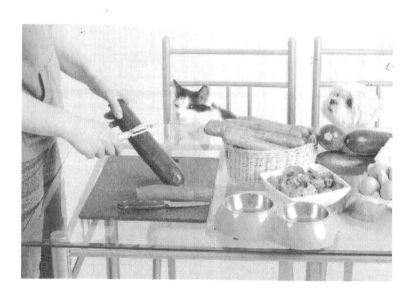

If you do some research of your own you will find that there are many who do not recommend cooking homemade cat food. Cooking can destroy the nutritional content of certain foods, altering the state of the proteins as well as the vitamins and minerals. The fact of the matter is that there is really no reason why you need to cook your cat's homemade food – it is usually done out of preference for the owner.

Many people worry about the potential for food-borne illness when feeding their cats a homemade food diet. It is important to note, however, that cats have an increased ability to fight off infection and their bodies are actually designed to process and digest raw foods. There is no harm in including some cooked meats in your cat's homemade diet but you should definitely consider feeding him a raw homemade diet. Because there is a great deal more support for raw cat food diets, most of the recipes you find in this book will be fore raw cat foods.

In the end, it is really a matter of preference how you choose to prepare your homemade cat food. There are many benefits associated with completely raw cat food diets, but some people simply aren't comfortable with preparing or feeding these diets. You can choose whether you want to leave your raw ingredients whole or you can choose to grind them. All that really matters is that you are using high-quality ingredients and they your homemade cat food recipe is properly formulated to meet your cat's nutritional needs. In the next chapter you will learn more about the details of homemade cat food including pros and cons as well as potential risks and important safety precautions to take.

Chapter Four: Risks and Rewards of Homemade Cat Food

Having cultivated a deeper understanding of what a raw homemade cat food diet looks like, you may be wondering whether it really is a better option for your cat. To help you decide you will find a list of pros and cons for homemade cat foods in this chapter as well as an overview of potential risks and safety precautions for this type of diet. This information will set you up to better understand the information in the following chapter about the components of a raw homemade cat food diet.

1. Pros and Cons of Homemade Cat Food

Now that you know a little bit more about what goes into homemade cat food you have a foundation of knowledge that will help you to better understand the pros and cons of homemade cat food. All types of cat food have their associated benefits and drawbacks so be sure to consider both sides of the story before you make your choice of what to feed your cat.

Below you will find an overview of the pros and cons for homemade cat food:

Pros for Homemade Cat Food

- A raw cat food diet more closely approximates the natural diet of wild cats than any other kind of food.

- Homemade cat food can be made with fresh, high-quality ingredients – you have control over what goes into your cat's food.

- Raw cat food diets are generally high in protein with moderate amounts of fat – commercial diets are often high in carbohydrate and low in nutritional value.

- Feeding cats a balanced homemade diet can improve overall nutrition and general health and wellness.

- A homemade cat food diet can improve your cat's digestion, helping him become more regular and making his stools smaller and less odorous.

- A balanced homemade diet can improve your cat's skin and coat health while also reducing the risk for food allergies and sensitivities.

- Eating raw meaty bones can improve your cat's dental health by preventing the buildup of plaque and tartar.

- Homemade cat food diets can be made to cater to your cat's preferences as well as his individual dietary or medical needs.

Cons for Homemade Cat Food

- Homemade cat food diets take more time and effort to prepare than pouring a bowl of kibble.

- The cost for homemade cat food can be much higher than for commercial cat food – high-quality dry food costs about $0.60 a day while raw cat food can cost anywhere from $1.00 to $3.50 a day.

- Raw homemade cat food does not have as long a shelf life as dry food – it must be refrigerated or frozen and generally used within 3 to 5 days.

- Homemade cat food made with raw meat and bones comes with a risk for food-borne illness – proper food safety procedures are required.

- Some cats simply do not like the texture of raw cat food – they may need to be transitioned over a period of weeks or months.

2. Potential Risks and Safety Precautions

As you have already learned, there are certain risks involved with preparing raw homemade cat food. These risks exist any time you are using raw ingredients like meat and eggs – it is not just for raw cat food that you need to be careful. Always handle raw meats with caution, being sure to wash your hands before and afterward and clean and disinfect your work surface thoroughly before and after. When it comes to storing raw cat food, always keep it in the refrigerator or freezer in an airtight container.

In addition to taking basic food handling safety precautions when preparing your cat's homemade food, you should also be sure to avoid certain ingredients that can be harmful or toxic for your cat. <u>The following ingredients are very dangerous for cats and you should never feed them as a treat or as part of your cat's diet</u>:

- Alcohol
- Artificial sweetener
- Cooked bones
- Chocolate
- Caffeine
- Coffee
- Citrus oil extracts
- Currants
- Dog food
- Egg yolk
- Grapes

- Garlic
- Iron supplements
- Macadamia nuts
- Milk (some cats)
- Moldy food
- Mushrooms
- Onions
- Persimmons
- Rhubarb leaves
- Sugar
- Tea

- Tobacco
- Yeast dough

If your cat accidentally ingests any of these foods, call the Pet Poison Helpline immediately at the following number: 1- (855) 764 – 7661.

Chapter Five: A Raw Diet for Your Cat

Having learned a little bit more about the types of homemade cat food as well as the associated pros and cons, you are now ready to learn the details for creating your own raw food diet for cats. In this chapter you will receive an overview of the kind of ingredients that should be included in a raw homemade diet as well as tips for supplementation and where to find your raw ingredients. This information will help to prepare you for the homemade cat food recipes provided in the next chapter of this cat food cookbook.

1. The Components of Raw Cat Food Diets

The beauty of a raw food diet for cats is that there is a wide variety of ingredients you can choose from. The main components, however, are raw meat and organs plus raw bones. It is important to keep in mind that different kinds of meat offer different nutritional compositions so you need to feed your cat a variety of foods to ensure that his diet is properly balanced.

Some of the best meats to use in raw cat food diets include chicken, turkey, Cornish hen, lamb, beef, and pork. These are the types of meat that you are most likely to find at your local grocery store. In some cases, you may also be able to find things like venison, duck, quail, bison, goat, rabbit, and pheasant but you can also order these foods online. As for organ meats, your best options are liver and kidney, though heart is also beneficial. One thing you need to remember is that you don't have to match the organs to the meat – you can use beef heart, chicken liver, and raw turkey all in one meal.

As for raw bones, there are several different ways you can go. In many cases you can offer your cat bone-in meats like poultry with edible, small bones. Some examples include Cornish hens, quail, and chicken wings, necks, ribs, or backs. These bone-in meats can be cut into smaller pieces with kitchen shears before offering them to your cat. Larger weight-bearing bones are harder for cats to break but you can try breaking them up with a hammer into more manageable pieces to feed them to your cat. Just be sure that any bones you offer your cat as part of a raw diet have meat on them.

Another thing you need to consider is the inclusion of fish in your raw diet for cats. Fish is a complete source of protein and it contains valuable fatty acids as well, but there are a variety of factors which make fish only good for cats in small amounts. Certain types of fish contain various toxins and histamines which can be dangerous for cats. If you do choose to incorporate fish into your raw diet, choose only wild-caught varieties in order to avoid antibiotics. If you feed sardines or other canned fish make sure they are packed in water without added salt.

If you feed your cat a balanced raw food diet you should not have to worry about supplementation. Even so, you will find some valuable information about using supplements in homemade cat food in the next section.

2. Supplements for Raw Food Diets

The type of raw diet you choose for your cat will determine whether or not you need to add any supplements. If you feed the frankenprey methodology, for example, your cat will receive a balance of nutrients simply through the variety of foods being offered. The only supplement you are likely to need with this type of methodology is omega fatty acids. If you prefer to grind your cat's food or if you want to stick to a single complete and balanced recipe, you will need to include certain supplements.

The supplements you are likely to need if you choose a single recipe for your cat's homemade raw diet include the

<u>following</u>:

- **Taurine** – An essential amino acid, taurine is best used in powdered form – it generally comes in 500mg capsules.

- **Vitamin E** – The best way to use this supplement is in dry capsules, though liquid capsules can be used if you can't find this vitamin in dry form.

- **Vitamin B Complex** – This vitamin is also best used in cry capsule form or you can find it powdered online.

- **Wild Salmon Oil** – Try to find capsules of wild salmon oil rather than a liquid in the bottle because it can go rancid quickly after opening. If you are grinding your cat's food, just add the entire capsule. Otherwise, pierce it and squeeze the oil out.

- **Salt** – It is best to use lite salt in your homemade cat food recipes. If you only have iodized table salt on hand, just use half the amount called for in the recipe.

- **Psyllium Husk Powder** – This ingredient is optional but it can help to add dietary fiber to your cat's diet.

You can try making food without this ingredient at first but if your cat becomes constipated, start using it.

Depending on your preference, you can create a homemade raw food diet for your cat and add these supplements individually. Another option is to find a nutritional supplement that is specifically designed to be used in homemade cat food recipes. These supplements contain all of the nutrients your cat needs to balance his nutrition when it is added to fresh meats and organs. Some examples of this kind of supplement include:

Alnutrin Supplements – This company offers high-quality nutritional supplements for homemade cat food in several different forms. The *Alnutrin with Calcium* product is made either with limestone or with eggshell powder for addition to a raw diet made without bones. For a raw diet made with meat and bones, the *Alnutrin Meat and Bone* supplement provides essential amino acids as well as vitamin E, copper, zinc, and more.

You can find these products online here:

www.knowwhatyoufeed.com/alnutrin_supplements.html

TC Feline – This company offers four different recipes for raw cat food premixes. The *TCfeline Original* recipe can be used in boneless meat recipes and it needs to be used with the addition of fresh liver. The *TCfeline PLUS with Beef Liver* is very similar to the original formula but it is made with New Zealand beef liver so you don't have to use fresh liver in your recipe. The *TCfeline PLUS with Chicken Liver* recipe can be combined with boneless meat of your choice and the *TCfeline Special Formula* can be used to make reduced protein diets for cats.

You can find these products online here:

www.tcfeline.com/tcfeline-canada/

Balance IT Feline – This company offers several different supplement formulas for homemade dog and cat food. The original *Balance IT Feline* recipe contains essential vitamins, minerals, and amino acids. The *Balance IT Feline-K* formula is intended for use with low-phosphorus homemade cat foods and the *Balance IT Feline-Ca* formula is designed for low-calcium homemade cat foods.

You can find these products online here:

www.balanceit.com/marketplace.html

3. Transitioning Your Cat Onto a Raw Food Diet

If you have ever tried switching your cat to a new food, you may already know that this can be a bit of a challenge. Making any sudden or drastic changes to your cat's diet can lead to gastrointestinal upset which can be very unpleasant for both you and your cat. In order to avoid problems, it is a good idea to slowly transition your cat onto a raw food diet if you choose to make the switch – you should also make sure that your vet knows about your choice to ensure that your cat doesn't have any medical problems that might be exacerbated by a change in what you are feeding him.

For picky eaters and for cats that are currently eating an all-dry diet, you may need to start by getting your cat used to eating canned food. Raw cat food has a very different texture and consistency from dry food, so your cat may need some extra time to get used to the change. You may also want to get your cat used to being fed at a certain time and eliminate free-feeding – you don't want to let raw food sit in your cat's bowl all day. If you currently free-feed your cat, start portioning his daily food into two or three meals and remove it about 30 minutes after you put it down so your cat gets used to eating right away.

To get your cat used to eating soft food, start mixing a little bit of it into your cat's wet food. If he doesn't seem to have any problem eating the wet food you can start feeding him most of his daily portion in wet food with a little of the dry food sprinkled on top. Even if your cat accepts the wet food immediately you don't want to make any major dietary changes too quickly. You should aim to transition your cat onto the wet food over a period of 5 to 7 days for the best results. When you do switch to wet food, make sure that it is high-quality, grain-free wet food.

If your cat still has trouble eating the wet food, try feeding him some dehydrated raw food or treats. These foods have a similar texture to dry food but they are made with raw ingredients and dehydrated. Putting some of this food on top of your cat's wet food may help. After your cat has gotten used to eating the wet food as his only food you can try feeding your cat some raw meat along with his canned cat food. Start with a few pieces of turkey or chicken liver. If your cat accepts it right away you can transition onto a raw food diet.

When you start feeding your cat raw food you'll want to make sure that you serve it warm. Do not cook the food, but place it in a plastic bag and float it in a bowl of warm water for 15 to 20 minutes to bring it up to body temperature for your cat. If your cat still needs encouragement to eat the raw food try sprinkling some organic catnip on it or crush up some dehydrated treats and sprinkle them on top. It may take a few days but if your cat refuses the food for a while he may eventually get hungry enough to eat it.

Chapter Six: Homemade Cat Food Recipes

One of the benefits of homemade cat food is that there are an unlimited number of ways you can combine your raw ingredients to create new and exciting flavors for your cat. Remember, you cannot just combine ingredients in random amounts and expect it to be complete and balanced for your cat – you need to follow recipes that have been approved by a vet or animal nutritionist. In this chapter you will receive an assortment of recipes. The raw recipes are complete and balanced but the cooked recipes should be fed in rotation to ensure nutritional balance.

1. Tips for Portioning Homemade Cat Food

When it comes to serving your cat's homemade cat food the method for portioning it out will be determined by the kind of food it is. For example, if you decide to follow the frankenprey methodology you will simply cut the raw ingredients into chunks and serve it up in a bowl or on a plate for your cat to enjoy. If you choose the grinding methodology, however, you may want to make things easier on yourself by shaping the ground mixture into patties or rolls for storage.

Below you will find a brief overview of options for storing and feeding your cat his homemade cat food:

Fresh Food – If you want your cat to receive the maximum nutritional benefit, prepare his food on the same day you intend to serve it. Simply cut the ingredients into pieces that your cat can chew on or gnaw on and serve them fresh.

Nuggets – If you choose to grind your cat's food you can shape the mixture into small nuggets and freeze them for easy storage. To make things easy for portioning, measure out the food and shape it into nuggets that each weigh ½ ounce or 1 ounce so you can just count the nuggets out when it comes time for feeding.

Patties or Rolls – Another way to store and serve ground cat food is to shape it into individual patties or rolls. If you choose to shape the mixture into patties, make each patty the proper size for one portion. If you choose to shape the ground mixture into rolls, make sure you know how thin or thick to slice it for the right portion size.

Baked Food – If you absolutely must cook your cat's homemade cat food, try mixing the ingredients together and then crumble the mixture onto a parchment-lined baking sheet. Bake the pieces at 350°F for 10 to 15 minutes until they are just dried then store them in an airtight container in the refrigerator for up to 5 days.

2. Raw Homemade Cat Food Recipes

<u>Recipes Included in this Section</u>:

Simple Raw Chicken Recipe

Ground Chicken and Eggs Dinner

Chopped Chicken and Veggies Recipe

Easy Ground Duck Dinner

Chopped Turkey and Pumpkin Recipe

Ground Beef and Bone Dinner

Turkey and Rabbit Recipe with Raw Bone

Ground Rabbit Dinner with Bones

Reduced-Protein Turkey Dinner

Raw Chicken Recipe without Bone

Simple Raw Chicken Recipe

Ingredients:

- 6 pounds raw chicken breasts and thighs
- 7 ½ ounces raw chicken liver
- 2 cups water
- 40g Alnutrin with Calcium supplement

Instructions:

1. Chop the chicken meat into pieces and toss it with the chopped chicken liver in a bowl.
2. Feed the mixture through a meat grinder, if desired, to create a uniform texture.
3. In a bowl, whisk together the water and the Alnutrin supplement until well combined.
4. Pour the mixture over the ground or chopped meat and toss until combined.
5. Portion the mixture as desired and freeze.

Ground Chicken and Eggs Dinner

Ingredients:

- 4 ½ pounds chicken thighs with skin and bone
- 7 ounces raw turkey or chicken livers
- 14 ounces raw chicken heart
- 1 cup bottled spring water
- 4 large egg yolks, whisked
- 4,000 mg wild salmon oil
- 200 mg vitamin B complex supplement
- 200 IU vitamin E supplement
- 2,000 mg taurine supplement

- 1 ½ teaspoons lite salt
- 1 tablespoon psyllium husk powder

Instructions:

1. Remove the skin from half of the chicken thighs but keep the fat.
2. Cut out about 25% of the bone from the chicken thighs and cut it into pieces.
3. Chop the chicken liver and chicken heart then toss it together with the chicken thigh meat.
4. Feed the mixture through a meat grinder and collect it in a large bowl.
5. Whisk together the water and egg yolks in a mixing bowl.
6. Pierce the salmon oil capsules and squeeze them into the bowl.
7. Open the vitamin B complex and vitamin E capsules and add the powder to the bowl then whisk until well combined.
8. Whisk in the taurine and salt then stir it all into your ground meat mixture.
9. Sprinkle in the psyllium husk powder and stir until well combined.
10. Portion the mixture as desired and freeze.

Chopped Chicken and Veggies Recipe
Ingredients:

- 4 ½ pounds chicken thighs
- 5 ounces raw chicken livers

- 15 ounces raw chicken hearts
- 1 small carrot, chopped or grated
- ½ cup frozen green peas, thawed
- 4 large egg yolks
- 2 cups water
- 40g Alnutrin with Calcium supplement

Instructions:

1. Remove most of the skin as well as the bone from the chicken thighs if they are not already boneless.
2. Chop the chicken thigh meat into bite-sized pieces.
3. Cut up the chicken hearts and livers and toss the pieces together with the thigh meat.
4. Cook the carrot and green peas as desired until very tender then mix into the meat and organ mixture along with the egg yolks.
5. In a medium bowl, whisk the Alnutrin supplement into the water.
6. Pour the liquid over the meat and veggie mixture and toss until well combined.
7. Portion out the mixture as desired and freeze.

Easy Ground Duck Dinner

Ingredients:

- 4 ½ pounds whole duck, dressed
- Chicken or turkey liver, as needed
- Chicken heart, as needed
- 1 cup bottled spring water
- 4 large egg yolks, whisked

- 4,000 mg wild salmon oil
- 200 mg vitamin B complex supplement
- 200 IU vitamin E supplement
- 2,000 mg taurine supplement
- 1 ½ teaspoons lite salt

Instructions:

1. Remove the skin from half of the duck, keeping the fat, and remove 25% of the bone then chop the meat.
2. Weigh the liver and heart that came with the bird and add enough chicken or turkey liver to equal 7 ounces and enough chicken heart to equal 14 ounces.
3. Chop the liver and heart then toss it together with the chopped duck meat.
4. Feed the mixture through a meat grinder and collect it in a large bowl.
5. Whisk together the water and egg yolks in a mixing bowl.
6. Pierce the salmon oil capsules and squeeze them into the bowl.
7. Open the vitamin B complex and vitamin E capsules and add the powder to the bowl then whisk until well combined.
8. Whisk in the taurine and salt then stir it all into your ground meat mixture.
9. Portion the mixture as desired and freeze.

Chopped Turkey and Pumpkin Recipe
Ingredients:

- 6 pounds raw dark-meat turkey, boneless
- 6.5 ounces raw chicken liver
- 2 cups water
- 40g Alnutrin with Calcium supplement
- 2 cups organic pumpkin puree

Instructions:

1. Chop the raw turkey meat into bite-sized pieces, including a small amount of the skin.
2. Cut the chicken liver into small pieces and toss it together with the chopped turkey.
3. In a large bowl, whisk together the water and the Alnutrin supplement until well combined.
4. Stir in the canned pumpkin then toss in the chopped turkey meat and liver.
5. Combine everything as thoroughly and evenly as possible.
6. Portion the mixture as desired and then freeze.

Ground Beef and Bone Dinner
Ingredients:

- 1 ½ pounds lean ground beef, raw
- 100 grams raw beef heart
- 100 grams raw chicken heart
- 100 grams raw chicken liver
- ½ cup bottled spring water
- 2 large egg yolks, whisked

- 2 tablespoons ground bone meal
- ½ teaspoon lite salt
- 2,000 mg taurine supplement
- 2,000 mg wild salmon oil
- 400 IU vitamin E supplement
- 200 mg vitamin B-complex supplement

Instructions:

1. Place the ground beef in a large bowl.
2. Chop the beef and chicken hearts along with the chicken livers and add to the bowl.
3. Toss the mixture together then feed it through a meat grinder and back into the bowl.
4. In a separate bowl, whisk together the water, eggs and bone meal.
5. Add the salt, taurine, salmon oil, vitamin E, and vitamin B-complex and whisk to combine.
6. Pour the liquid into the bowl with the ground meat and toss it all together.
7. Portion the mixture as desired and freeze.

Turkey and Rabbit Recipe with Raw Bone

Ingredients:

- 2 ¼ pounds fresh turkey breast, bones cut out and reserved
- 2 pounds fresh rabbit meat, bones cut out and reserved
- 14 ounces raw chicken heart
- 7 ounces raw chicken or turkey liver

- 2 cups water
- 4 large egg yolks, whisked
- 4,000 mg salmon oil
- 800 IU vitamin E supplement
- 200 mg vitamin B-complex supplement
- 1 ½ teaspoons light salt
- 4 teaspoons psyllium husk powder

Instructions:

1. Remove about half of the skin from the turkey breast and cut it into chunks.
2. Cut the rabbit into bite-sized pieces, keeping most of the skin on.
3. Combine the raw bones with the liver and heart in a bowl then feed it through a meat grinder.
4. Pour the water into a mixing bowl and whisk in the egg yolks, salmon oil, vitamin E, vitamin B-complex, and salt.
5. Stir in the psyllium husk powder then toss in the ground bone mixture along with the chopped meats.
6. Portion the mixture as desired and freeze.

Ground Rabbit Dinner with Bones

Ingredients:

- 8 pounds raw rabbit (meat, organs, and bone)
- 2 cups water
- 32g Alnutrin Meat & Bone supplement

Instructions:

1. Cut the rabbit into pieces and feed it all through a meat grinder into a large bowl.
2. In a separate bowl, whisk together the water and the Alnutrin supplement.
3. Pour the liquid into the bowl with the ground meat mixture and stir until very well combined.
4. Portion the mixture as desired and freeze.

Reduced-Protein Turkey Dinner

Ingredients:

- 2 pounds lean ground turkey breast
- 1 cup bottled spring water
- 2 large egg yolks, whisked
- 4,500 mg calcium carbonate powder
- 4,000 mg wild salmon oil
- 4,000 mg taurine supplement
- 400 IU vitamin E supplement
- 200 mg vitamin B complex supplement
- 2 cups pumpkin puree
- 1 cup grass-fed butter, softened

Instructions:

1. Place the ground turkey in a large bowl.
2. In a separate bowl, whisk the water and eggs.
3. Add the calcium carbonate, taurine, salmon oil, vitamin E, and vitamin B-complex and whisk to combine.
4. Pour the liquid into the bowl with the ground meat and toss it all together.

5. In a saucepan, combine the pureed pumpkin with the softened butter over medium heat.
6. Cook until the butter is melted and the mixture is warmed through then add to the meat mixture.
7. Toss everything together and let cool to room temperature.
8. Portion the mixture as desired and freeze.

Raw Chicken Recipe without Bone

Ingredients:

- 3 bones chicken thighs and drumsticks, bones removed
- 14 ounces raw chicken heart
- 7 ounces raw chicken or turkey liver
- 2 cups water
- 4 large egg yolks, whisked
- 3 tablespoons bone meal
- 4,000 mg salmon oil
- 800 IU vitamin E supplement
- 200 mg vitamin B-complex supplement
- 1 ½ teaspoons light salt
- 4 teaspoons psyllium husk powder
- 2 tablespoons unflavored gelatin

Instructions:

1. Remove about half of the skin from the chicken and cut it into chunks.
2. Combine the liver and heart in a bowl then feed it through a meat grinder.

3. Pour the water into a mixing bowl and whisk in the egg yolks, bone meal, salmon oil, vitamin E, vitamin B-complex, and salt.
4. Stir in the psyllium husk powder and gelatin then toss in the ground organ mixture along with the chopped meats.
5. Portion the mixture as desired and freeze.

3. Cooked Homemade Cat Food Recipes

Recipes Included in this Section:

High-Protein Chicken and Spinach Recipe

Sautéed Rabbit Stew

Reduced-Protein Duck and Egg Recipe

Chicken and Broccoli Stew

Cornish Hen and Oat Dinner

Beefy Potato Cat Casserole

Creamy Salmon Pasta

Chicken, Lentils and Rice Recipe

Sardine and Chicken Liver Dinner

Turkey and Pasta Recipe

High-Protein Chicken and Spinach Recipe

Ingredients:

- 3 ¼ ounces boneless, skinless chicken breast
- 2 tablespoons steamed brown rice
- 2 teaspoons canola oil
- 2 tablespoons frozen spinach, thawed
- 2 tablespoons grated apple
- 3.7 grams Balance IT Feline supplement

Instructions:

1. Heat the canola oil in a small skillet or saucepan.
2. Chop the chicken into bite-sized pieces and add them to the pan.
3. Sauté the chicken until it is cooked through.
4. Stir in the remaining ingredients and cook until just warmed through
5. Let the mixture cool for a few minutes before serving to your cat.

Sautéed Rabbit Stew

Ingredients:

- 1 teaspoon olive oil
- ½ pound fresh rabbit meat, bone and skin removed
- ¼ teaspoon dried parsley
- ¼ teaspoon dried rosemary
- 1 cup peeled and diced sweet potato, carrot, turnip, and celery

Instructions:

1. Heat the olive oil in a small saucepan over medium-high heat.
2. Cut the rabbit into bite-sized chunks.
3. Add the rabbit to the saucepan and sauté until the meat is just browned.
4. Sprinkle with parsley and rosemary then pour in the vegetable stock.
5. Bring the mixture to a boil then simmer until the rabbit is cooked through.
6. Add the remaining ingredients then cover and simmer on very low heat for 30 to 45 minutes until the veggies are tender.
7. Let the mixture cool for a few minutes before serving to your cat.

Reduced Protein Duck and Egg Recipe
Ingredients:

- 2 ½ large egg whites, beaten
- 1 ounce duck breast meat
- ¼ cup quick-cooking oats, cooked
- 3 tablespoons mashed sweet potato
- 1 teaspoon canola oil
- ¼ cup summer squash, diced
- ¼ cup frozen spinach, thawed and drained
- 4.2 grams Balance IT Feline supplement

Instructions:

1. Heat the canola oil in a small skillet over medium heat.
2. Add the beaten egg whites and cook until set, stirring as needed.
3. Stir in the duck meat and cook until browned.
4. Add the remaining ingredients and sauté for 2 to 3 minutes until just heated through.
5. Let the mixture cool slightly before feeding.

Chicken and Broccoli Stew
Ingredients:

- 2 pounds boneless, skinless chicken breast, chopped
- 80 grams chicken liver, cooked and chopped
- 1 ½ cups water

- 1 ounce chopped broccoli
- 4 grams unflavored gelatin
- 14 grams Alnutrin with Calcium supplement
- 1,200 mg salmon oil

Instructions:

1. Combine the chicken breast and chicken liver in a small saucepan.
2. Add just enough water to cover the meat then simmer, covered, on lo wheat for 30 minutes until the chicken is cooked through.
3. In another saucepan, steam the broccoli until tender then let cool.
4. Pour the chicken, chicken liver, and liquid into a bowl and cool for 10 minutes.
5. Stir in the steamed broccoli along with the gelatin, supplement powder, and salmon oil.
6. Transfer the ingredients to a food processor, puree.
7. Divide the mixture into portions and chill for 3 hours until the gelatin is set before serving.

Cornish Hen and Oat Dinner
Ingredients:

- 2 cup old-fashioned oats
- 1 tablespoon canola oil
- 1 pound fresh Cornish game hen meat, chopped
- 2 large egg whites, beaten

- ¼ cup mashed sweet potato
- 2 tablespoons kelp powder
- 2 tablespoons bone meal
- 50 mg taurine supplement

Instructions:

1. Cook the oats according to the directions on the package and set aside to cool.
2. Heat the oil in a medium saucepan over medium-high heat.
3. Add the Cornish game hen meat and cook until browned, stirring often.
4. Remove the meat to a bowl and reheat the skillet using the cooking grease from the game heat.
5. Add the egg whites and scramble until they are cooked through.
6. Stir the cooked game hen back into the saucepan along with the mashed sweet potato, kelp powder, bone meal, and taurine supplement.
7. Add the oats and stir to combine then remove from heat and cool for 10 minutes.
8. Serve the meal as desired and store the leftovers in the fridge.

Beefy Potato Cat Casserole
Ingredients:

- 1 pound lean ground beef

- 1 teaspoon brewers yeast
- ½ teaspoon powdered calcium supplement
- 1/8 teaspoon psyllium husk powder
- 100 mg taurine supplement
- 3 cups parboiled potatoes, peeled and sliced thin
- ½ cup cottage cheese, pureed
- 2 to 3 tablespoons grated parmesan cheese
- ¼ cup unsweetened almond milk

Instructions:

1. Preheat the oven to 350°F and lightly grease a casserole dish with cooking spray.
2. Cook the ground beef until it is browned and cooked through then drain the fat.
3. Stir in the brewers yeast along with the calcium supplement, psyllium husk powder, and taurine supplement.
4. Spread the ground beef mixture in the bottom of the casserole dish.
5. Arrange the potato slices over the beef and sprinkle with cottage cheese and parmesan.
6. Pour in the milk then bake for 15 minutes until the cheese is melted.
7. Remove from the oven and cool before serving.

Creamy Salmon Pasta
Ingredients:

- 1 pounds boneless salmon fillet (skin okay)
- 1 cup whole-grain elbow pasta
- ¼ cup frozen spinach, thawed and drained
- ¼ cup shredded cheddar cheese
- 4 tablespoons kelp powder
- 100 mg taurine supplement

Instructions:

1. Brush the salmon fillet with olive oil and broil in the oven until it is just cooked through.
2. Cook the pasta in a pot of lightly salted water until al dente, about 8 to 10 minutes, then drain.
3. Combine the cooked pasta with the spinach, cheese, kelp powder and taurine in a food processor.
4. Flake the salmon into the food processor.
5. Pulse the mixture several times until it is chopped and thoroughly combined.
6. Cool the mixture then serve as desired.

Chicken, Lentils and Rice Recipe
Ingredients:

- 1 ½ pounds whole roaster chicken, skin removed
- 1 ½ cups white rice, steamed
- 1 cup cooked red lentils, drained
- 100 mg taurine supplement

Instructions:

1. Chop the chicken and place it in a large stockpot.
2. Fill the pot with enough water to cover the chicken then bring to a boil.
3. Reduce heat and simmer until the chicken is cooked through then drain and shred the meat.
4. Place the shredded chicken in a food processor then add the cooked lentils and rice.
5. Pulse the mixture several times to combine then pulse in the taurine supplement.
6. Allow the mixture to cool before serving to your cat.

Sardine and Chicken Liver Dinner

Ingredients:

- 1/3 cup white rice, uncooked
- 2/3 cups water
- 2 cans of sardines in oil, drained and chopped
- 2 whole chicken livers, cooked and chopped
- 1 large egg, scrambled or boiled
- ¼ cup fresh chopped parsley
- 100 mg taurine supplement

Instructions:

1. Combine the water and rice in a small saucepan and bring to a boil, covered.
2. Reduce heat and simmer for 20 minutes then turn off the heat and let the rice absorb the rest of the water.

3. Meanwhile, combine the sardines, chicken livers, egg, and parsley in a food processor.
4. Pulse the mixture until well combined then pulse in the rice.
5. Add the taurine supplement and pulse to combine.
6. Cool the mixture and then serve as desired.

Turkey and Pasta Recipe

Ingredients:

- 1 pound lean ground turkey breast
- 1 cup whole-grain elbow pasta
- 2 large egg whites, beaten
- ½ cup plain nonfat Greek yogurt
- 1 teaspoon dried parsley
- ½ teaspoon bone meal
- 100 mg taurine supplement

Instructions:

1. Cook the ground turkey in a skillet until browned then drain the extra grease.
2. Bring a pot of lightly salted water to boil then add the pasta and cook to al dente, about 8 to 10 minutes.
3. Drain the pasta and set it aside.
4. Spoon the turkey into a food processor then reheat the skillet and cook the egg whites until set.

5. Add the cooked egg and pasta to the food processor along with the yogurt, parsley, bone meal, and taurine.

6. Pulse the mixture until well combined but not quite pureed.

7. Cool the mixture if needed and serve as desired.

Chapter Seven: Homemade Treat Recipes

Not only can you create your own homemade cat food, but you can also make homemade treats! Homemade cat treats are great because you do not have to worry about making them complete and balanced. Making your own cat treats is a great way to supplement your cat's nutrition, however – they can also be a fun way to bribe your cat into eating raw cat food if he tends to be a little bit picky. In this chapter you will find an assortment of cat treat recipes including everything from homemade jerky treats to baked cat snacks. So get to baking!

Recipes Included in this Section:

Tuna Cat Crackers
Catnip Kitty Cookies
Chicken Jerky Bites
Sunflower Oat Treats
Beefy Bites
Chicken Biscuits
Tasty Tuna Tidbits
Cheesy Cat Treats
Baked Liver Bites
Canned Food Cookies

Tuna Cat Crackers

Ingredients:

- 1 cup whole-wheat flour
- 1 cup yellow cornmeal
- 5 to 6 tablespoons water
- 1 (6-ounce) can tuna in water, undrained

Instructions:

1. Preheat the oven to 350°F and line a baking sheet with parchment paper.
2. Combine the flour, cornmeal and water in a bowl and stir well.
3. Flake the tuna into the bowl and add the liquid from the can.
4. Stir until everything is well combined then roll out to ¼-inch thickness.
5. Cut the dough into bite-sized treats and arrange on the baking sheet.
6. Bake for 20 minutes or so until golden brown and store in an airtight container.

Catnip Kitty Cookies

Ingredients:

- 1 cup whole-wheat flour
- ¼ cup oat or soy flour
- 6 tablespoons powdered milk
- 2 tablespoons ground flaxseed
- 1 teaspoon dried catnip
- 1/3 cup unsweetened almond milk

- 2 tablespoons melted coconut oil
- 1 tablespoon molasses
- 1 large egg, beaten

Instructions:

1. Preheat the oven to 350°F and line a baking sheet with parchment paper.
2. Combine the flours, powdered milk, flaxseed, and catnip in a bowl and stir well.
3. Stir in the almond milk, coconut oil, molasses and egg until everything is well combined.
4. Roll the dough out to ¼-inch thickness.
5. Cut the dough into bite-sized treats and arrange on the baking sheet.
6. Bake for 20 minutes or so until golden brown and store in an airtight container.

Chicken Jerky Bites

Ingredients:

- 1 ½ pounds boneless, skinless chicken breast
- ¼ cup olive oil
- 2 teaspoons salt
- 1 teaspoon dried rosemary
- 1 teaspoon dried parsley

Instructions:

1. Preheat the oven to 200°F.
2. Whisk together the olive oil, salt, rosemary and parsley in a mixing bowl.

3. Trim the excess fat from the chicken and cut it into thin slices with the grain.
4. Toss the chicken strips with the spice mixture until evenly coated.
5. Spread the strips out on a wire cooling rack set over a rimmed baking sheet.
6. Bake for 2 hours until the strips are dried.
7. Cool the jerky strips and cut or break into bite-sized pieces.
8. Store the treats in airtight containers in the fridge.

Sunflower Oat Treats

Ingredients:

- 1 cup whole-wheat flour
- 1 cup old-fashioned oats
- ¼ cup ground flaxseed
- ¼ cup sunflower seeds
- ½ cup diced apple
- ¼ cup grated carrot
- 1 cup all-natural peanut butter
- 1 cup molasses or honey

Instructions:

1. Preheat the oven to 200°F.
2. Combine the flour, oats, flaxseed, sunflower seed, apples and carrots in a mixing bowl.
3. Melt the peanut butter in a microwave-safe bowl for 15 seconds on high heat.

4. Pour the peanut butter and molasses over the mixture in the bowl and stir until well combined.
5. Shape the mixture into a dough ball then roll it out.
6. Cut the dough into bite-sized pieces and arrange them on a parchment-lined baking sheet.
7. Bake for up to 2 hours until the treats are firm and dried.
8. Store in an airtight container after cooling completely.

Beefy Bites

Ingredients:

- 3 small jars beef baby food
- 1 ½ cups wheat germ
- 1 tablespoon water or canned tuna liquid

Instructions:

1. Combine all of the ingredients in a mixing bowl and stir until well combined.
2. Cover a plate with parchment paper.
3. Spoon the mixture onto the plate in rounded ¼ teaspoons.
4. Cook the treats in the microwave on high for 5 to 8 minutes until they are firm.
5. Store the treats in an airtight container in the fridge.

Chicken Biscuits

Ingredients:

- 1 ½ cups cooked chicken breast, shredded
- ½ cup low-sodium chicken broth
- 1 tablespoon coconut oil
- 1 cup whole-wheat flour
- ¼ cup yellow cornmeal

Instructions:

1. Preheat the oven to 350°F and line a baking sheet with parchment.
2. Combine the chicken, chicken broth and coconut oil in a food processor.
3. Pulse the ingredients several times to combine.
4. Add the whole-wheat flour and cornmeal then pulse until it forms a dough.
5. Roll the dough into a ball then roll it out to ¼-inch thickness.
6. Cut the dough into bite-sized pieces and arrange them on the baking sheet.
7. Bake for 16 to 20 minutes until crisp and dried.
8. Cool completely and store in an airtight container.

Tasty Tuna Tidbits

Ingredients:

- 1 (6-ounce) can tuna in water, drained
- 1 large egg white, cooked and chopped
- ¼ cup water
- ½ cup whole-wheat flour

- ¼ cup yellow cornmeal

Instructions:

1. Preheat the oven to 350°F and line a baking sheet with parchment.
2. Flake the tuna into a bowl and stir in the egg white and water.
3. Stir in the whole-wheat flour and cornmeal until it forms a dough.
4. Knead the dough into a ball then roll it out to ¼ inch thickness.
5. Cut the dough into bite-sized pieces and arrange them on the baking sheet.
6. Bake for 15 to 20 minutes until dried and crisp.
7. Store in airtight containers in the refrigerator.

Cheesy Cat Treats

Ingredients:

- ¾ cups shredded cheddar cheese
- ¼ cup grated parmesan cheese
- ¼ cup plain Greek yogurt, nonfat
- ¾ cups whole-wheat flour
- ¼ cup yellow cornmeal

Instructions:

1. Preheat the oven to 350°F and line a baking sheet with parchment.
2. Stir together the yogurt and cheese in a mixing bowl.
3. Add the whole-wheat flour and cornmeal then stir into a dough.

4. If needed, add a little water until the dough sticks together then roll into a ball.
5. Roll the dough out to ¼-inch thick and cut into bite-sized pieces.
6. Arrange the treats on the baking sheet and bake for 20 to 25 minutes until crisp and dried.
7. Cool completely then store in an airtight container.

Baked Liver Bites

Ingredients:

- ½ cup chicken livers, cooked and chopped
- ¼ cup warm water
- 1 ¼ cups whole-wheat flour
- ¼ cup mashed sweet potato
- 1 tablespoon coconut oil

Instructions:

1. Preheat the oven to 325°F and line a baking sheet with parchment or foil.
2. Place the cooked chicken liver in a blender with the water and blend until pureed.
3. In a mixing bowl, stir together the whole wheat flour and coconut oil.
4. Stir in the blended liver and the mashed sweet potato.
5. Knead the mixture into a ball then roll it out to ¼-inch thickness.
6. Cut the dough into small bite-sized treats and arrange them on a baking sheet.
7. Bake for 10 to 12 minutes until crisp and dried.

8. Store in an airtight container in the refrigerator.

Canned Food Cookies

Ingredients:

1 can of paté cat food

Instructions:

1. Preheat the oven to 350°F and line a baking sheet with parchment paper.
2. Scoop the contents of the cat food can onto a plate.
3. Cut the loaf of cat food into ¼-inch slices then cut them into quarters.
4. Shape the pieces into round cookies and place them on the baking sheet.
5. Bake for 25 to 30 minutes until the cookies are dried and crispy.
6. Cool completely and store in an airtight container.

Chapter Eight: Frequently Asked Questions

    In reading this book you have received a wealth of information about different kinds of diets for cats. Not only did you receive an introduction to commercial cat food diets and a list of pros and cons for homemade cat food, but you have also learned the details about different kinds of homemade cat food and their associated benefits. By now you should have the information you need to decide whether homemade cat food is right for your cat but you may still have some general questions about feeding your cat. In this chapter you will find a list of frequently asked questions to satisfy your curiosities.

Q: *Is it safe to feed kittens a raw food diet?*

A: Raw food is great for all cats, including kittens! What many cat owners do not realize is that kittens and adult cats do not have significantly different nutritional needs. Kittens do, however, need more calories than adult cats to fuel their healthy growth and development – it is best if those extra calories come from protein. You can definitely feed your kittens a raw food diet, just be sure to cut it into pieces small enough for them to chew. You should also be sure to feed them a variety of raw foods so they do not get used to one thing and grow up into picky eaters.

Q: *How much should I be feeding my cat on a raw food diet?*

A: Determining how much to feed your cat on a raw food diet can be tricky, especially if you make the food yourself. Commercial cat food packages come with feeding instructions but if you make your own cat food you'll have to determine the right amount yourself. Your best bet is to start with a complete and balanced product and then to feed your cat a certain amount based on his weight.

The easiest way to calculate how much your cat needs to eat is to multiply his weight in pounds by 16 – this will tell you how much your cat weighs in ounces (ex: 7 pounds x 16 = 112 ounces). Then, take that number and multiply it by 2%, 3%, or 4% depending on your cat's needs (these percentages converted to a decimal are 0.02, 0.03, and 0.04). It is a good idea to start with 3% and to monitor your cat's weight for a few weeks. If he gains too much weight, reduce to 2% - if he loses weight, increase to 4%. Keep in mind that kittens will need to eat more than adult cats – free-feeding is generally the best option for kittens.

Q: *Aren't raw bones dangerous for cats?*

A: You have probably heard that chicken bones are bad for cats and dogs because they can splinter and cause serious damage. What you may not realize, however, is that this rule applies only to cooked bones. Chicken bones, and bones from other kinds of meat, become more brittle when they are cooked which increases the risk for breakage and splintering. Raw bones, on the other hand, are soft enough that your cat can actually chew them up and swallow them. Raw bones provide some significant nutritional benefits for cats so they are an important part of a homemade diet.

Q: *Should I grind my raw cat food or serve it whole?*

A: There is a great deal of controversy regarding this subject in the world of homemade cat food. Some animal experts recommend grinding raw cat food to create a more cohesive product and to reduce the risk for intestinal blockages caused by raw bones. In reality there are pros and cons for both options so carefully consider the information provided in Chapters 3 and 4 to make your own decision.

Q: *Do I have to use organic ingredients in my homemade cat food?*

A: The beauty of homemade cat food is that you can choose the ingredients that go into it. You do not necessarily have to choose organic ingredients, but there are many benefits to doing so. Organic produce is not exposed to any chemical pesticides or herbicides which might be transferred to your cat. Organic meats such as grass-fed beef and cage-free chicken are raised without antibiotics or hormones which makes them a more natural protein source for your cat. All you really have to do, however, is purchase the highest quality ingredients you can afford. If that means using inorganic produce, fine – it is more important to fee your cat a balanced diet than to worry about organic versus inorganic ingredients.

Q: *What if my cat is allergic to chicken?*

A: If your cat is allergic to chicken there are plenty of other meat options you can use in your homemade cat food diet. Turkey is the option that is most similar to chicken but if your cat is allergic to chicken he may also have problems with other poultry. Try feeding your cat some beef, venison, lamb, or pork to see how he handles it. You can also offer some fresh fish or other seafood but just be sure that you keep an eye on his fat intake.

Q: *Why can't I just feed my cat a bowl of raw meat?*

A: In nature, wild cats subsist mainly on a diet of raw meat. They kill their prey and eat the meat raw. What you may not realize is that wild cats also eat some of the bones of their prey as well as the stomach contents which may contain plant matter, depending on the type of prey. By consuming raw bones and some plant matter in addition to different kinds of meat, wild cats receive a fairly balanced diet. If you just feed your cat a bowl of raw meat, he could be missing out on some important nutrients.

For example, raw bones are rich in calcium which your cat needs to support a healthy skeletal system. If you feed your cat the same kind of meat all the time (with no additional supplements), he will probably not get the kind of balanced diet he needs to remain healthy. Many proponents of the raw food diet for cats recommended alternating between several different recipes to ensure nutritional balance and to keep the cat from getting used to one recipe and refusing any other kind of food.

Q: *What is the best way to cook homemade cat food?*

A: If you choose to feed your cat a cooked homemade diet there are certain cooking methods that are better than others. Generally speaking, you want to choose a cooking method that doesn't require the addition of too much cooking oil and you want to preserve as much of the nutritional integrity of your ingredients as you can. Poaching (or boiling) is one of the best cooking methods for chicken and other poultry – baking is also a good choice. You can choose to cook your ingredients separately or bake them after you have compiled and blended your recipe.

Q: *How much fiber should my cat get?*

A: As you have already learned in reading this book, cats are obligate carnivores and they have no biological need for carbohydrate in their diet. Still, there are certain benefits that come with dietary fiber in a diet for cats. Not only does dietary fiber help to promote digestive health but, for unknown reasons, it also seems to help manage weight and hypoglycemia, especially in older cats. Dietary fiber for cats should come from digestible carbohydrates and it should make up no more than 10% of the cat's diet.

Q: *How often should I feed and water my cat?*

A: Your cat needs to have constant access to an unlimited supply of fresh water. Not only is water important for hydration but it also helps to support healthy digestion for your cat. Each cat is different, but it is generally recommended that you feed your cat twice a day. Divide your cat's daily ration into two portions and offer one in the morning and one in the evening. Many cats do not eat their whole meal at once – they prefer to graze throughout the day. This is perfectly fine as long as your cat is not overeating.

Q: *What should I do if my cat is overweight?*

A: If your cat is carrying around too much weight you should take him to the vet to confirm that he needs to shed some pounds. Some cats are simply larger than others – it is possible for a 20-pound cat to be completely healthy in terms of weight and body composition. If your cat does need to lose weight, however, you can simply reduce the amount of food you offer your cat but still follow the same feeding schedule with the same number of daily feedings. Another option is to switch to a low-calorie cat food. Just be sure that it provides for your cat's protein needs to help him maintain lean muscle mass.

Index

A

AAFCO	4, 23, 26, 27, 114
absorb	6, 18, 84
Alnutrin	52, 61, 64, 67, 70, 77
amino acids	4, 5, 6, 52, 53
animal feed	26
animal nutritionists	8
animal products	4, 5
arginine	5

B

Balance IT	53, 74, 76
balanced	3, 2, 7, 27, 35, 37, 43, 48, 49, 50, 57, 86, 99, 101, 102, 117
beef	37, 38, 48, 53, 68, 80, 92, 101, 102
benefits	1, 36, 40, 42, 57, 98, 100, 101, 103
bloating	30
Blue Buffalo	31
bodyweight	14
bones	11, 24, 34, 35, 36, 37, 38, 43, 44, 46, 48, 52, 69, 72, 100, 101, 102
brands	18, 20, 31
bread	7

C

Calcium	11, 52, 61, 64, 67, 77
calorie	14, 105
Canidae	31
canned food	23
capsules	51, 62, 63, 65, 66
carbohydrate	4, 7, 8, 9, 10, 28, 29, 30, 42, 103
carnivores	4, 103

Castor & Pollux 32

cat food 3, 1, 2, 3, 17, 18, 19, 20, 21, 22, 23, 24, 25, 26, 27, 28, 31, 33, 40, 41, 42, 43, 45, 47, 49, 52, 55, 56, 86, 98, 99, 100, 105, 117

cat treat 86

chew 35, 58, 99, 100

chicken 28, 29, 37, 38, 48, 56, 61, 62, 64, 65, 67, 68, 69, 72, 74, 77, 83, 84, 90, 93, 96, 100, 101, 103

chicken meal 29

chickpeas 8, 23, 30

Chocolate 46

coat 6, 24, 43

commercial 6, 7, 16, 17, 19, 20, 21, 30, 31, 32, 33, 36, 42, 43, 98

complete proteins 5

condition 15, 24, 36

cooking 17, 18, 21, 22, 28, 29, 39, 76, 78, 80, 103

Copper 12

corn 23, 29

Cornish hen 48

crude fiber 27

D

dehydrated 25, 55, 56, 116

development 10, 12, 13, 26, 99

diarrhea 30

diet 3, 1, 2, 3, 6, 7, 8, 9, 30, 33, 34, 35, 36, 37, 39, 41, 42, 43, 46, 47, 48, 49, 50, 51, 52, 54, 55, 56, 99, 100, 101, 102, 103, 114, 115, 117

dietary fiber 7, 23, 51, 103

digest 5, 6, 18, 30, 35, 40

digestive issues 30

disinfect 45

dry matter 22, 27

duck 37, 38, 48, 65, 76

E

Earthborn Holistic 32

eggs 4, 5, 8, 45, 68, 71

energy 4, 6, 7, 10, 11, 14, 15, 29

enzymes 21, 25

essential amino acids 5

essential fatty acids 6, 29

extruder 18

F

fat 4, 5, 6, 8, 9, 15, 26, 27, 29, 34, 42, 62, 65, 80, 90, 102

feeding 14, 15, 25, 26, 35, 36, 37, 39, 40, 54, 55, 56, 58, 59, 76, 98, 99, 100, 102, 104, 114, 115

feline 35, 114, 115

fillers 29

fish 4, 5, 8, 28, 49, 102

flaxseed 30, 89, 91

food 3, 1, 2, 3, 7, 14, 16, 17, 18, 19, 20, 21, 22, 23, 24, 25, 26, 27, 28, 29, 30, 31, 32, 33, 34, 35, 36, 37, 39, 40, 41, 42, 43, 44, 45, 46, 47, 48, 49, 50, 51, 52, 53, 54, 55, 56, 57, 58, 59, 77, 82, 83, 84, 85, 86, 92, 93, 97, 98, 99, 100, 101, 102, 103, 104, 114, 115, 116, 117

frankenprey 34, 35, 36, 37, 50, 58, 114

Fromm 32

G

gas 30

glucose 4, 7, 10

gluten 8, 29, 30

grain-free 23, 30, 55

grains 7, 17, 23

gravy 22

grinding 17, 34, 35, 51, 58, 100

growth 10, 13, 18, 26, 99

guaranteed analysis 22, 27, 28

H

health 3, 1, 3, 9, 24, 43, 103, 114, 117

heat 22, 24, 71, 75, 76, 78, 79, 83, 84, 91

holistic 23

Holistic Select   32

homemade   3, 1, 2, 3, 7, 33, 34, 39, 40, 41, 42, 43, 44, 45, 47, 49, 50, 51, 52, 53, 57, 58, 59, 86, 98, 100, 101, 103, 114, 117

Honest Kitchen   32

housecat   15

I

I and Love and You   32

immune system   24

ingredients16, 17, 18, 21, 22, 23, 24, 25, 26, 27, 28, 29, 33, 34, 35, 40, 42, 45, 47, 48, 55, 57, 58, 59, 74, 75, 76, 77, 92, 93, 101, 103, 117

Iodine   13

Iron   12, 46

J

jerky   86, 90

joints   24

K

kibble   21, 23, 25, 43

kittens   14, 26, 99, 100, 114

L

lamb   48, 102

life stage   27

list 27, 28, 29, 31, 32, 41, 98

liver   34, 37, 38, 48, 53, 56, 61, 62, 65, 67, 68, 69, 72, 77, 96

lose weight   104

M

macronutrients   4, 8, 9

Magnesium 11

meal 7, 28, 29, 35, 36, 37, 38, 48, 68, 72, 78, 79, 85, 104

meat4, 5, 7, 8, 17, 22, 28, 29, 34, 35, 36, 37, 38, 44, 45, 48, 49, 52, 53, 56, 61, 62, 63, 64, 65, 66, 67, 68, 69, 70, 71, 72, 75, 76, 77, 78, 83, 100, 101, 102, 116

medical 43, 54

Merrick 32

micronutrients 4, 9

middlings 8, 29

milk 14, 80, 89

minerals 4, 9, 11, 26, 39, 53

moisture 18, 22, 24, 25, 28, 29

muscle 4, 11, 105

N

natural 21, 23, 26, 34, 36, 42, 91, 101

Natural Balance 32

Nature's Variety 32

needs 2, 3, 6, 8, 9, 10, 14, 15, 16, 24, 27, 43, 52, 53, 56, 99, 102, 104

nutrients 3, 4, 6, 9, 14, 18, 21, 23, 26, 27, 50, 52, 102

nutrition 2, 3, 4, 15, 16, 35, 43, 52, 86, 114, 115, 116

nutritional adequacy 27

nutritional deficiencies 3, 117

nutritional needs 3, 2, 3, 16, 24, 27, 40, 99, 117

Nutro 32

O

oil 29, 46, 51, 62, 65, 68, 69, 71, 72, 74, 75, 76, 77, 78, 82, 84, 89, 90, 93, 96, 103

omega-3 6

omega-6 6

organ 34, 48, 64, 72

organic 56, 67, 101

Organix 32

Orijen 32

overweight 15, 104

P

pasta	7, 82, 85
paté	22, 97
peas	23, 30, 64
pet foods	16, 17, 26, 29
Pet Poison Helpline	46, 115
pet store	16, 20
Phosphorus	11
picky eaters	35, 55, 99
plant	4, 6, 30, 102
plant matter	102
plaque	21, 36, 43
pork	37, 38, 48, 102
portions	38, 77, 104
Potassium	12
pregnant	14
prey	7, 34, 36, 102, 114
Primal Pet Foods	32
problems	3, 9, 54, 102, 117
proportions	18
pros and cons	3, 1, 2, 40, 41, 42, 47, 98, 101, 117
protein	4, 5, 8, 9, 11, 12, 22, 26, 27, 29, 42, 49, 53, 99, 101, 105

Q

quality	8, 16, 18, 20, 23, 26, 27, 29, 30, 31, 32, 40, 42, 43, 52, 55, 101
questions	33, 98

R

rabbit	37, 38, 48, 69, 70, 75
raw	3, 2, 17, 21, 22, 24, 25, 26, 34, 35, 36, 37, 40, 41, 42, 43, 44, 45, 47, 48, 49, 50, 52, 53, 54, 55, 56, 57, 58, 61, 62, 64, 67, 68, 69, 70, 72, 86, 99, 100, 102, 114, 115, 117
raw ingredients	17, 21, 25, 47
recipe	3, 2, 18, 40, 50, 51, 53, 103
requirements	2, 7, 26, 27
research	3, 6, 26, 39

rice   7, 30, 74, 83, 84

S

schedule	37, 104
skin	6, 12, 24, 34, 38, 43, 62, 64, 65, 67, 69, 72, 75, 82, 83
Sodium	12
soy	23, 29, 89
Stella & Chewy's	32
sterilization	22
stew	22
supplements	7, 17, 21, 46, 49, 50, 52, 102
sweet potatoes	8, 23, 30
switch	3, 1, 54, 55, 105, 117

T

tapioca	23, 30
tartar	21, 36, 43
Taste of the Wild	32
Taurine	5, 51
TCfeline	53
teeth	11, 21, 36
tissue	4, 12
toxic	46
treats	3, 2, 55, 56, 86, 88, 89, 90, 91, 92, 95, 96, 117
turkey	29, 37, 38, 48, 56, 62, 65, 67, 69, 71, 72, 85

V

vegetables	7
venison	48, 102
vet	54, 57, 104
Vitamin B	51
Vitamin E	10, 51
vitamins	4, 6, 9, 10, 26, 39, 53

W

wean   14
weight   14, 15, 28, 49, 99, 103, 104
Wellness   32
wet food   55
wheat   23, 29, 77, 88, 89, 91, 92, 93, 94, 95, 96
whole prey   35
whole-grain   30, 82, 85
wild   7, 34, 35, 36, 42, 49, 51, 62, 65, 68, 71, 102
wild cats   7, 34, 36, 42, 102
Wysong   32

Z

Ziwipeak   32

References

"AAFCO Methods for Substantiating Nutritional Adequacy of Dog and Cat Foods." AAFCO.org. <http://www.aafco.org/Portals/0/SiteContent/Regulatory/Committees/Pet-Food/Reports/Pet_Food_Report_2013_Midyear-Proposed_Revisions_to_AAFCO_Nutrient_Profiles.pdf>

"Answers: Raw Feed All of Those Kittens!" Feline Nutrition Foundation. <http://feline-nutrition.org/answers/answers-raw-feed-all-of-those-kittens>

Dion, Tracy. "A Prey Model Raw (PMR)/Whole Prey Feeding Guide." CatCentric. <http://catcentric.org/nutrition-and-food/raw-feeding/a-frankenprey-and-whole-prey-feeding-guide/>

"Do Dogs and Cats Need Carbohydrates in their Diet?" Petnet. <http://www.petnet.io/pet_health_blogs/do-dogs-and-cats-need-carbohydrates-in-their-diet#.V0hbZpErIuU>

Edgar, Julie. "Homemade Cat Food and Raw Cat Food." PetMD. <http://pets.webmd.com/cats/guide/homemade-cat-food-and-raw-cat-food>

"Essential Amino Acids for Your Cats." Petnet. <http://www.petnet.io/pet_health_blogs/essential-amino-acids-for-your-cats#.V0hYHZErIuU>

"Foods to Avoid Feeding Your Cat." PetEducation.com. <http://www.peteducation.com/article.cfm?c=1&aid=1029>

"How are Dry Pet Foods Made?" PetMD. <http://www.petmd.com/dog/nutrition/evr_multi_dry_pet_food#>

"How to Transition Your Cat to a Raw Meat Diet." Feline Nutrition Foundation. <http://feline-nutrition.org/nutrition/how-to-transition-your-cat-to-a-raw-diet>

"Myth: Homemade, Cooked Diets are Better, Safer Alternative to Raw." Rawfed.com. <http://rawfed.com/myths/cookedfood.html>

"Omega Fatty Acids: Sources, Effects & Therapeutic Uses in Cats." PetEducation.com. <http://www.peteducation.com/article.cfm?c=1+1400&aid=665>

"Pet Poison Helpline." Pet Poison Helpline. <http://www.petpoisonhelpline.com/>

"Rad Cat Raw Diet." RadFood.com. <http://www.radfood.com/education/feeding>

"Raw Cat Food Types and 5 Recommendations." Pet Food Chat. <http://petfood.chat/catfood/raw-types/>

Schultze, Kymythy. "Your Cat's Nutritional Requirements: The Basics." Kymythy.com. <http://www.kymythy.com/articles12.html>

Temple, Courtney. "Freeze Dried and Dehydrated Pet Food." Pet360.com. <http://www.pet360.com/dog/nutrition/freeze-dried-and-dehydrated-pet-food/mPaSU2XXvEacl-ixDSE2JQ>

"Types of Meat to Use in Homemade Cat Food." A House Full of Cats. <http://www.a-house-full-of-cats.com/meat.html>

"What Goes into Making Wet Pet Food?" PetMD. <http://www.petmd.com/dog/nutrition/evr_multi_wet_pet_food#>

"Your Cat's Nutritional Needs." National Research Council. <http://dels.nas.edu/resources/static-assets/materials-based-on-reports/booklets/cat_nutrition_final.pdf>

Feeding Baby
Cynthia Cherry
978-1941070000

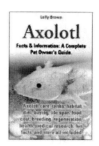

Axolotl
Lolly Brown
978-0989658430

Dysautonomia, POTS
Syndrome
Frederick Earlstein
978-0989658485

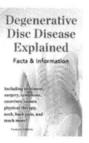

Degenerative Disc
Disease Explained
Frederick Earlstein
978-0989658485

Sinusitis, Hay Fever,
Allergic Rhinitis Explained
Frederick Earlstein
978-1941070024

Wicca
Riley Star
978-1941070130

Zombie Apocalypse
Rex Cutty
978-1941070154

Capybara
Lolly Brown
978-1941070062

Eels As Pets
Lolly Brown
978-1941070167

Scabies and Lice Explained
Frederick Earlstein
978-1941070017

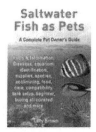

Saltwater Fish As Pets
Lolly Brown
978-0989658461

Torticollis Explained
Frederick Earlstein
978-1941070055

Kennel Cough
Lolly Brown
978-0989658409

Physiotherapist, Physical
Therapist
Christopher Wright
978-0989658492

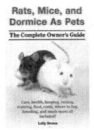

Rats, Mice, and Dormice
As Pets
Lolly Brown
978-1941070079

Wallaby and Wallaroo Care
Lolly Brown
978-1941070031

Bodybuilding Supplements
Explained
Jon Shelton
978-1941070239

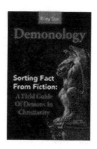

Demonology
Riley Star
978-19401070314

Pigeon Racing
Lolly Brown
978-1941070307

Dwarf Hamster
Lolly Brown
978-1941070390

Cryptozoology
Rex Cutty
978-1941070406

Eye Strain
Frederick Earlstein
978-1941070369

Inez The Miniature Elephant
Asher Ray
978-1941070353

Vampire Apocalypse
Rex Cutty
978-1941070321